Spotlight on™ Reading & Listening Comprehension Level 2

Understanding Everyday Information

by Paul F. Johnson & Carolyn LoGiudice

Skills	Ages
■ reading	■ 11 and up
■ listening	**Grades**
	■ 6 and up

Evidence-Based Practice

According to *Put Reading First: The Research Building Blocks for Teaching Children to Read* (2003):

■ Instruction in comprehension can help students understand, remember, and communicate with others about what they read.

■ Good readers use metacognitive strategies to think about and have control over their reading.

■ Teacher questioning improves students' learning from reading because it gives them a purpose for reading, focuses their attention on what they are to learn, helps them think actively as they read, encourages them to monitor their comprehension, and helps them review content and relate what they've learned to what they already know.

■ Teaching students to ask their own questions improves their active processing of text and their comprehension.

The activities in this book incorporate the above principles and are also based on expert professional practice.

LinguiSystems

LinguiSystems, Inc.
3100 4th Avenue
East Moline, IL 61244

FAX: 800-577-4555
Phone: 800-776-4332
E-mail: service@linguisystems.com
Web: linguisystems.com

Printed in the U.S.A.
ISBN 978-0-7606-0731-2

About the Authors

Paul F. Johnson, B.A., and **Carolyn LoGiudice**, M.S., CCC-SLP, are editors and writers for LinguiSystems. They have collaborated to develop several publications, including *Story Comprehension To Go*, *No-Glamour Sequencing Cards*, and *Spotlight on Reasoning & Problem Solving*. Paul and Carolyn share a special interest in boosting students' language, critical thinking, and academic skills.

In their spare time, Paul and Carolyn enjoy their families, music, gourmet cooking, and reading. Paul, a proud father of three children, also enjoys bicycling, playing music, and spending rare moments alone with his wife, Kenya. Carolyn is learning to craft greeting cards and spoil grandchildren.

Cover design by Jeff Taylor
Editing and page layout by Karen Stontz

Table of Contents

Introduction

Spotlight on Reading & Listening Comprehension was developed in 2005 to provide controlled reading materials for improving both overall and specific comprehension skills. Six separate booklets presented passages with readabilities that varied from grades 2.0 through 4.9 along with follow-up comprehension questions. Each booklet focused on one of these key reading comprehension skills:

- Characters & Actions
- Comparing & Contrasting
- Figurative Language & Exclusion
- Making Inferences & Drawing Conclusions
- Paraphrasing & Summarizing
- Sequencing & Problem Solving

Requests for a similar approach to reading comprehension skill-building that would be more appealing to older students has resulted in *Spotlight on Reading & Listening Comprehension, Level 2*. Not only are the readabilities of the passages increased in this series, but the content and visual elements are designed to appeal to older students reading below grade level.

Each booklet includes stories and comprehension questions for detecting the main idea, identifying details, and thinking about the vocabulary and semantics in the passage. In addition, each booklet includes comprehension questions for a specific skill area. This particular booklet features questions that require students to understand everyday information in what they have read. The other five booklets focus on these skill areas:

- Comparing & Contrasting
- Figurative Language
- Fact & Opinion
- Paraphrasing & Summarizing
- Making Inferences & Drawing Conclusions

The readability of the passages is controlled, based on the Flesch-Kincaid readability statistics. These statistics were revised in 2002; the new statistics yield a higher grade level in most cases than the previous ones. The range in readability is from grade levels 4.0 through 6.9. Each booklet includes eleven passages with the following readability ranges:

- Passages 1-3   Readability 4.0-4.9
- Passages 4-7   Readability 5.0-5.9
- Passages 8-11   Readability 6.0-6.9

The question pages for each passage also ask students to formulate questions about what they have read. The last task for each passage is a related writing prompt.

Use these passages for groups of students or individuals. Photocopy or print the material from the CD so each student has a copy. Encourage your students to highlight or underline key information as they read each passage and to jot down any questions they have.

Research proves that repeated readings improve reading comprehension and that three reads are usually sufficient repetition for a student to grasp the content, assuming a passage is at or below the student's reading competency level. We recommend training students to read a passage three times for adequate comprehension before trying to answer the comprehension questions.

The reading comprehension questions are similar to those found on classroom and national reading comprehension tests. Have your students read each possible answer for the multiple-choice questions before they select their answers.

As you present information to your students, model your own reading comprehension strategies. Talk about ways to rescan a passage to find key information and other tips that will help your students improve their reading competence and confidence.

We hope you will find *Spotlight on Reading & Listening Comprehension, Level 2* a welcome resource to help students understand and find satisfaction in what they read.

Paul and Carolyn

Story 1

Thank you for calling the West Valley School District. Please listen carefully to the following options. Some numbers may have changed since your last visit. Press *0* at any time during this call to speak to the operator. Press *1* if you would like to hear the options in English. Press *2* for Spanish.

If you are calling to talk to a staff member, press *1*. You will be sent to the main directory. Enter the first few letters of the first or last name of the person you wish to reach and your call will be forwarded to that person.

If you would like to speak to Principal McLarty, press *2*. Press *3* if you would like to leave a message for the principal. Press *4* for sports information. Press *5* for bus schedules and delays. If there are possible weather delays, watch TV channel 63 or listen to KBER 620 AM. Finally, press *6* for lunch menus and prices.

If you would like to hear these options again, press *star* on your keypad. To return to the main menu, press the *pound sign*. Again, thank you for calling West Valley School District. We're home to the fighting Pirates and the best students in the world! Have a great day!

Main Idea and Details

1. Which best describes this message?

    a. a phone answering system message

    b. an announcement from the prinicipal

    c. a message on a Web site

2. What is the name of the school district mentioned in this story?

    a. West Lake School District

    b. West Valley School District

    c. Valley Vale School District

3. Which button do you need to press if you want to hear the message in Spanish?

    a. 1

    b. 2

    c. 3

Vocabulary and Semantics

4. In the story, it says **Press *1* if you want to hear the options in English**. What's another word for **options**?

    a. choices

    b. numbers

    c. members

5. The message tells you to **Please listen carefully**. Which word is the opposite of **carefully**?

    a. closely

    b. casually

    c. carelessly

Understanding Everyday Information

6. What could you do if you had something to say to the principal but didn't need to talk to him immediately?

    a. get sports information

    b. leave a message

    c. hang up

7. What would be the best thing to do if there might be bus delays because of bad weather?

    a. watch TV or listen to the radio

    b. press star to hear the options again

    c. wait for the bus to see if it shows up

8. Can you reach a school staff member through this system?

    a. yes

    b. no

Asking Questions

Ask a question about telephone answering services.

Writing and Discussion Prompt ································

Imagine you have an answering system like this where you live. What message would people hear when they call? What options would they have?

Story 2

Photo courtesy of iStockphoto.com © Michael Knight

What if aliens came to Earth and brought a great gift? That's exactly what happens in the new movie *Earth Station 2020*. The problem is, the gift isn't as perfect as it seems at first.

The Earth is facing some big problems in 2020. There isn't enough energy and food for everyone. Many people are out of work and wars are common. Then one day a huge spaceship blocks out the sun. It lands in New York's Central Park and sits there quietly for days. Thousands of people gather around the ship. After a week, a giant door opens and three aliens walk out. They say four simple words: "We have the answer."

The answer they bring seems to solve all of the world's problems, but their gift comes at a large price. I won't spoil the movie by telling you what that price is. You'll have to see it to find out.

If you're looking for a fun movie to see on a summer afternoon, *Earth Station 2020* is a good choice. It is full of great action and interesting ideas. It probably won't win any awards, but the two hours will fly by! I guarantee you'll want to see it again and again.

Main Idea and Details

1. Which best describes this message?

   a. a video game review

   b. a movie review

   c. an advice column

2. What is the name of the movie in this story?

   a. *Earth Station 2020*

   b. *Battle for Earth 2020*

   c. *Spaceship New York*

3. Where does the spaceship land?

   a. Washington, D.C.

   b. Central Park

   c. Yosemite National Park

Vocabulary and Semantics

4. The story says that **wars are common**. Which of these is not another word for **common**?

   a. everyday

   b. frequent

   c. rare

5. The aliens said, "**We have the answer**." Which of these is another word for **answer**?

   a. figure

   b. solution

   c. problem

Understanding Everyday Information

6. What happens right after the spaceship lands?

    a. Thousands of people gather around it.

    b. Three aliens walk out.

    c. People begin attacking the ship.

7. Which sentence best describes the story of this movie?

    a. It is based on real events.

    b. It is about a famous person's life.

    c. It is a made-up story.

8. Which sentence best describes how the reviewer feels about the movie?

    a. The movie should win a lot of awards.

    b. It is entertaining and fun to watch.

    c. People should not see this movie.

Asking Questions

Ask a question about something that might happen in the movie.

Writing and Discussion Prompt ·······························

Imagine you are one of the people gathered around the ship. Describe what you see.

Story 3

Third Avenue Courts welcomes you! Our goal is to be a safe, fun place for everyone to play. We thank you in advance for following these rules and playing fairly.

1. All players must sign in at the front desk and receive a court pass. No one is allowed on the courts without clearly displaying a court pass.
2. No foul language, teasing, threatening, or trash talking is allowed at any time. Let your game do the talking, not your mouth!
3. Gym shoes must be worn at all times. No street shoes or bare feet are allowed.
4. Proper gym attire is required at all times. Gang colors, team uniforms, and street clothes are prohibited on the courts.
5. Backpacks, bags, and personal items are not allowed in the gym. Those items must be left outside the facility or securely stored in the locker room.
6. When the courts are full and teams are waiting to play, the winning score of a game may not exceed 20 points. Game losers must leave the court and go to the end of the waiting list for the court.

Anyone breaking these rules will be asked to leave. First-time rule breakers will be banished for one week. If you break the rules twice, you will not be allowed back for one month. Three-time rule breakers are no longer welcome at Third Avenue Courts.

Readability 4.7
Copyright © 2007 LinguiSystems, Inc.

Main Idea and Details

1. Which best describes this message?

   a. how to play basketball

   b. basketball schedule

   c. basketball court rules

2. What must you have before you can play?

   a. a court pass

   b. a uniform

   c. a note signed by a parent

3. If people are waiting to play, teams can play to a maximum score of _____.

   a. 10

   b. 15

   c. 20

Vocabulary and Semantics

4. Some kinds of clothing are prohibited. What is another way to say **prohibited**?

   a. not allowed

   b. required

   c. encouraged

5. **The first time you break the rules, you are banished for one week**. What is another way to say **you are banished for one week**?

   a. You have to clean the locker rooms for a week.

   b. You can't play at the courts for one week.

   c. For the next week, you have to be at the courts every day.

Understanding Everyday Information

6. Why are there so many rules at these courts?

    a. to prevent problems and keep it a safe place to play

    b. to make it easy to kick people out

    c. to discourage people from playing there

7. Which of these is a good reason for not letting people bring backpacks to the courts?

    a. Backpacks are heavy and people might get injured when they carry them.

    b. People might bring in weapons or other things that would cause trouble.

    c. Most backpacks are old and they wouldn't look good around the courts.

8. What happens if you break the rules three times?

    a. You are no longer allowed at the courts.

    b. You aren't allowed at the courts for one month.

    c. You aren't allowed at the courts for one week.

Asking Questions

Ask a question about the rules for this court.

Writing and Discussion Prompt ·····································

Do you think all of these rules are fair? Explain your answer.

Story 4

Photo courtesy of iStockphoto.com © Stephen Walls

Some people are happy with a simple hamburger made of ground beef. If you're a little more adventurous, follow these directions to make world-class spicy burgers.

Start with a pound of good quality ground beef or ground chuck roast. Put the meat in a large bowl because you're going to be mixing in a lot of ingredients. Add a quarter cup of steak sauce and two tablespoons of hot sauce. If you like extra spicy burgers, add more hot sauce. Then add a few shakes of salt and pepper and a teaspoon of garlic powder. This may sound weird, but the last thing to add is a splash of white milk. Finally, make sure your hands are clean and mix everything together.

Divide the mixture to make three patties. Put the burgers on a hot grill and cook for five minutes per side. Don't smash the burgers down while they're cooking or they will be dry. Remove the burgers from the grill and serve them with your favorite toppings. Make sure you have plenty of napkins on hand while you eat these juicy, spicy burgers!

Main Idea and Details

1. Which best describes this message?

    a. rules

    b. a recipe

    c. a review

2. How much meat do you need to make this recipe?

    a. five pounds

    b. a half pound

    c. one pound

3. What shouldn't you do while the burgers are cooking?

    a. smash them down

    b. flip them over

    c. mix them together

Vocabulary and Semantics

4. This recipe is for people who want to be adventurous. Someone who is **adventurous** probably likes to _____.

    a. play it safe

    b. do things that are very dangerous

    c. try new things

5. The recipe tells you to **divide the mixture**. What is another word for **divide**?

    a. mix

    b. separate

    c. combine

Understanding Everyday Information

6. Why is it important that you use a large bowl?

    a. You need room to mix together a lot of ingredients.

    b. You might make more later.

    c. Hamburgers rise like bread dough.

7. Which ingredient might some people think is weird?

    a. steak sauce

    b. white milk

    c. hot sauce

8. What should you do before you mix all the ingredients together?

    a. serve with your favorite toppings

    b. turn on the grill

    c. make sure your hands are clean

Asking Questions

Ask a question about making hamburgers.

Writing and Discussion Prompt............................

Would you like to eat hamburgers made using this recipe? Why? If you had to add two more ingredients to this recipe, what would you add and why?

Story 5

Photo courtesy of istockphoto.com © Matthew Stanzel

Something is happening in our hallways that must stop now. We need to work together to solve this problem because it affects us all. The halls of our school are not trash cans, but many students must think they are.

I have seen people every day simply throwing their papers and garbage on the floor. It's disgusting to walk through trash every day, and it makes us all look like pigs. We all want to be treated like adults, but sometimes we act like babies. Who will respect us if we can't take care of ourselves and our own garbage?

When papers fall out of your locker, pick them up and throw them away. Don't just leave them there for someone to slip on. Our school custodians work hard to keep our hallways clean, and we don't need to make their jobs more difficult.

It's embarrassing that I even have to write about this, but something must be done. If we don't start taking care of things ourselves, we will all suffer. If you see people throwing trash on the floor, please tell them to clean it up. I hope we can work together to solve this ugly problem.

Main Idea and Details

1. Which best describes this message?

    a. directions

    b. a class schedule

    c. an opinion column

2. What problem is this person writing about?

    a. littering in the halls

    b. keeping lockers clean

    c. talking back to teachers

3. What does this person say students should do if they see others throwing trash on the floor?

    a. tell a teacher about it

    b. tell the person to pick up the trash

    c. pick it up yourself

Vocabulary and Semantics

4. Which animal does this writer compare students to?

    a. pigs

    b. horses

    c. rats

5. This story says that **custodians work hard to keep our hallways clean**. What is another word for **custodians**?

    a. family members

    b. janitors

    c. instructors

Understanding Everyday Information

6. Which of these is not a reason that littering is a problem?

    a. Littering makes students look like babies.

    b. Litter looks disgusting.

    c. Litter doesn't bother some people.

7. How might litter be dangerous?

    a. Someone could slip on a piece of paper and fall.

    b. The principal could get mad and yell loudly.

    c. The trash cans might get too full.

8. How would this writer describe people who litter the halls?

    a. lazy and careless

    b. forgetful and friendly

    c. helpful and generous

Asking Questions

Ask a question about littering in school hallways.

Writing and Discussion Prompt ·······································

What is something that happens in your school that you would like to change?

How could it be changed?

Story 6

Congratulations on purchasing your new computer desk. If you follow these directions carefully, you will enjoy your desk for many years.

Before You Begin

You will need an adjustable wrench and a large area to assemble your desk. Carefully open the box and spread the pieces on a clean, flat surface. Check the item list to make sure you have all the correct pieces.

Assembly

Flip the top (part A) upside down and line up the right leg support (part B) with the holes in the top. Use the adjustable wrench to attach the bolts (parts C) through the leg support and into the top. Do not tighten the bolts all the way until the final step. Do the same with the inside leg support (part D) and the left leg support (part E).

Next, have another person help you flip over the desk. Tighten all of the bolts with the adjustable wrench. Then have that person help you move the desk to the place where you will use it. Finally, attach the plastic corner protectors, slide the drawer into place, and get to work!

Readability 5.5
Copyright © 2007 LinguiSystems, Inc.

Main Idea and Details

1. Which best describes this message?

    a. safety tips

    b. an opinion column

    c. directions

2. Which tool do you need to put this desk together?

    a. a drill

    b. a hammer

    c. a wrench

3. How many people does it take to put this desk together?

    a. one

    b. two

    c. three

Vocabulary and Semantics

4. These are directions for assembling a desk. Which of these is not a way to say **assembling**?

    a. putting together

    b. destroying

    c. building

5. The directions tell you to **use the adjustable wrench to attach the bolts**. What is another word for **attach**?

    a. remove

    b. bend

    c. fasten

Understanding Everyday Information

6. Where would be a good place to spread out all the pieces?

    a. on a small table

    b. on a clean floor

    c. on the grass

7. What should you do after you spread out the pieces but before you start to put the desk together?

    a. tighten all of the bolts

    b. have another person help you flip over the top

    c. make sure you have all of the correct pieces

8. Why do the directions say you need another person?

    a. to help flip over the desk and move it

    b. to hold the bolts in place

    c. to attach the leg supports

Asking Questions

Ask a question about putting together a piece of furniture.

Writing and Discussion Prompt.................................

Give me directions for building your favorite sandwich. What ingredients will I need? What steps will I need to follow?

Readability 5.5
Copyright © 2007 LinguiSystems, Inc.

Story 7

Photo courtesy of iStockphoto.com © christopher o driscoll

It looks like we're in for a gray day at the beginning of the workweek, but plenty of sunny skies and warm temperatures are on their way! You'll want to make some outdoor plans for the upcoming weekend. Here's the full forecast:

Monday

Showers and thunderstorms are likely in the morning. The clouds should clear up by late afternoon. Expect a high of 85.

Tuesday

We'll see sunny skies with a few clouds throughout the day. Temperatures should warm up to the low 90s by late afternoon.

Wednesday

There is a slight chance of morning showers in the northern part of the region. Everyone else should see partly cloudy skies and a high of 88.

Extended Forecast

Look for warm, sunny weather late in the week with highs in the low 90s. The weekend should be sunny and clear with highs in the mid 80s. No rain is expected again until early next week.

Main Idea and Details

1. Which best describes this message?

   a. a sports report

   b. a weather report

   c. an information sheet

2. What is the first day of this weather forecast?

   a. Monday

   b. Wednesday

   c. Saturday

3. Which day early in the week would probably be best for a picnic?

   a. Monday

   b. Tuesday

   c. Friday

Vocabulary and Semantics

4. **Showers and thunderstorms are likely on Monday morning**. What is another way to say that?

   a. There is a good chance of rain Monday morning.

   b. Monday morning will probably be sunny.

   c. You should stay home from school on Monday.

5. The story says that **We're in for a gray day at the start of the workweek**. What is a **gray day**?

   a. a sad day

   b. a sunny day

   c. a cloudy day

Understanding Everyday Information

6. Considering the weather forecast, which activity would be best to do during the weekend?

   a. swimming

   b. cleaning your room

   c. studying for a test

7. Imagine this is a forecast for New York City. Which month might it be for?

   a. December

   b. February

   c. July

8. Which word describes what the weather forecast is for early next week?

   a. rainy

   b. sunny

   c. clear

Asking Questions

Ask a question about predicting the weather.

Writing and Discussion Prompt ······························

Describe the weather today. What outdoor activities would be good to do today?
What activities would not be good to do? Why?

Story 8

The Kennedy Community Center announces its summer activity lineup. We have great classes, sports, and programs again this year! Here are a few highlights:

Classes

Crafting classes are always a big hit when school is out, and we have plenty of them. We'll start off the summer with bead jewelry, quilting, and paper crafts. Later, we'll offer classes in clay sculpture and kite making.

Sports

You can't have summer without baseball. Kennedy offers leagues for ages 5 through 50 and beyond. Of course, swimming and diving programs continue through the summer months. There are also special golf, wall climbing, and paintball outings.

Programs

Day camp is always the highlight of our summer, and this year we've added another great opportunity. The Kennedy Center now has a sleepover camp in Morgan Woods. Weeklong camping programs are open to kids in fifth through tenth grades.

Come join us for another amazing summer. We can't wait to see you again!

Main Idea and Details

1. Which best describes this message?

    a. program information

    b. travel directions

    c. a weather forecast

2. Which sport is not offered?

    a. swimming

    b. soccer

    c. golf

3. Where is the sleepover camp located?

    a. Fredrick Forest

    b. Kennedy Center

    c. Morgan Woods

Vocabulary and Semantics

4. The story says **crafting classes are always a big hit**. What does that mean?

    a. They are popular.

    b. They are difficult.

    c. They are very easy.

5. This story talks about the summer activity lineup. What is another word for **lineup**?

    a. schedule

    b. time

    c. camp

Understanding Everyday Information

6. What kind of camp is not offered through the Kennedy Center?

   a. a weeklong camp

   b. a day camp

   c. an all-summer camp

7. Which of these describes the ages for Kennedy Center programs?

   a. grade school

   b. high school

   c. almost all ages

8. Which sports can you participate in at any time during the summer months?

   a. swimming and diving

   b. paintball and rock climbing

   c. T-ball and flag football

Asking Questions

Ask a question about activities students do during the summer.

Writing and Discussion Prompt.................................

Which sports or programs mentioned in the message would you be most interested in doing? Why? Which would you be least interested in and why?

Story 9

Thank you for signing up for a Carlyle City Library System card. A library card is your key to all the library system has to offer. Here are some benefits of being a library member:

Borrowing Materials

You can check out books, magazines, DVDs, and CDs for three weeks. Books and magazines can be renewed once for another three-week period. DVDs and CDs must be returned after three weeks and cannot be renewed. Late fees are ten cents per day for up to two weeks. After that time, you will be charged for the replacement price of the item.

Internet and Computer Use

Library members can reserve up to three hours of computer and Internet time per week. We guarantee a computer will be available for the time you have reserved.

Special Requests

The Carlyle City Library System is linked with all other library systems in the state. If another library has a book or material you'd like, let us know. You can search for and reserve materials at our Web site. We'll let you know when the items arrive, and you can check them out for the regular term.

Thanks for becoming a member of your public library!

Readability 6.4
Copyright © 2007 LinguiSystems, Inc.

Main Idea and Details

1. Which best describes this message?

   a. a library card

   b. directions to the library

   c. library information

2. Which library system is this message about?

   a. Carlyle City

   b. Granite City

   c. West Carlyle

3. How many hours of Internet time can library card holders reserve per week?

   a. three hours

   b. four hours

   c. as many hours as you want

Vocabulary and Semantics

4. This message says **some materials can be renewed**. What does **renewed** mean?

   a. owned

   b. returned

   c. checked out again

5. If you reserve Internet time, the library guarantees a computer will be available. What is another word for **guarantees**?

   a. denies

   b. promises

   c. closes

Understanding Everyday Information

6. How much are overdue fines?

    a. one dollar per day

    b. five dollars per week

    c. ten cents per day

7. Which materials cannot be renewed?

    a. books

    b. DVDs

    c. magazines

8. What can the library do if it doesn't have a material you want?

    a. get it from another library in the state

    b. buy it for you

    c. nothing

Asking Questions

Ask a question about using the library.

Writing and Discussion Prompt ·······························

What are your favorite things to check out of the library? What things do you never check out of the library?

Story 10

Are you ready for the greatest video game adventure of your life? If that's what you're looking for, then the new game *Extreme Hideaway 2* is probably not your best bet.

In this new game, you play as Carl Piven, a secret agent with an impossible mission. You'll need to travel the world, collect secrets, and solve lots of puzzles. The problem is there isn't much of a point to all of the running around you need to do. The mission is so impossible, you'll probably never even complete it.

Sure, the graphics look great and some of the puzzles are challenging, but it just doesn't all work together. Even though Carl Piven is supposed to be a secret agent, he's kind of a wimp and very boring. In the first game of the series, *Extreme Hideaway*, you could play as one of several different characters. It's too bad they didn't continue that approach in the sequel.

The bottom line is that *Extreme Hideaway 2* isn't terrible, but it isn't a classic either. Maybe you should just save your money for version three of the game. I hope they get that one right.

Main Idea and Details

1. Which best describes this message?

   a. a news story

   b. a video game review

   c. movie information

2. What is the name of the game reviewed?

   a. *Secret Agent 2*

   b. *Hideout Extreme*

   c. *Extreme Hideaway 2*

3. What is the name of the secret agent in the game?

   a. Carl Piven

   b. Carl Perkins

   c. Sal Piven

Vocabulary and Semantics

4. The review describes the secret agent in the game as a wimp. What is a **wimp**?

   a. a weak, cowardly person

   b. an exciting hero

   c. an interesting character

5. This review describes the mission as impossible. Which of these is the opposite definition of something that is **impossible**?

   a. It can't be done.

   b. It can be done easily.

   c. It can partially be done.

Understanding Everyday Information

6. Which part of the game does the reviewer like?

    a. the graphics

    b. the main character

    c. the title

7. What is the biggest difference between the original game and *Extreme Hideaway 2*?

    a. You could play as one of several different characters in the first game.

    b. The new game is a lot better.

    c. The puzzles are easier in the new game.

8. Which best describes how the reviewer feels about *Extreme Hideaway 2*?

    a. It is a complete waste of time.

    b. The main character is the best part of it.

    c. It isn't terrible, but it isn't great.

Asking Questions

Ask a question about playing video games.

Writing and Discussion Prompt··

Imagine you could help design a video game. Where would your game take place? Who would your main character be? What would the character have to do?

Story 11

Photo courtesy of istockphoto.com © Karen Phillips

Dear Darla:

My best friend in the world is not a perfect person at all. She's had some trouble at school, and she's even had some difficulties with the law. My friend has made some bad decisions, but she's a caring, intelligent, thoughtful, fun person. She's asked me to stay overnight with her several times, but my parents won't let me go. They think my friend is a bad influence, and they don't want me to stay with her or her family. How can I change what my parents think about my friend, especially since she's someone I really admire?

Megan

Dear Megan:

First of all, you need to remember that your parents' main job is to keep you safe. Sometimes their decisions don't seem to make sense, but they usually make those decisions because they feel they are protecting you. The solution to your problem might be as simple as asking your friend to spend the night with you a few times. Maybe if your parents get to know your friend a little better, they'll forget about her reputation and see her as a person. Spending more time with someone is usually the best way to get to know her better. Good luck!

Darla

Readability 6.7

Main Idea and Details

1. Which best describes this message?

    a. a news story

    b. rules

    c. an advice column

2. What won't Megan's parents let her do?

    a. stay overnight at her friend's house

    b. talk to her friend at school

    c. let Megan's friend stay at their house

3. Which of the following hasn't been a problem for Megan's friend?

    a. the law

    b. school

    c. Darla

Vocabulary and Semantics

4. Which pair of words means about the same thing?

    a. difficulties/solutions

    b. problems/difficulties

    c. perfect/trouble

5. Megan describes her friend as thoughtful. Which word doesn't mean the same as **thoughtful**?

    a. caring

    b. friendly

    c. insensitive

Understanding Everyday Information

6. What problem does Megan have?

    a. Her parents don't like her best friend.

    b. Her best friend is in trouble with the law.

    c. Her parents and best friend argue a lot.

7. How does Darla feel about Megan's parents?

    a. She thinks Megan's parents are wrong.

    b. She understands how Megan's parents feel.

    c. She thinks Megan's parents are being unfair.

8. What solution does Darla suggest?

    a. Invite the friend over so the parents can get to know her.

    b. Sneak over to the friend's house.

    c. Stop being friends with this person to keep the parents happy.

Asking Questions

Ask a question about being a good friend.

Writing and Discussion Prompt ·····································

Do you agree with the advice Darla gave Megan? Explain why you feel that way.

Answer Key

Story 1
1. a
2. b
3. b
4. a
5. c
6. b
7. a
8. a

Story 2
1. b
2. a
3. b
4. c
5. b
6. a
7. c
8. b

Story 3
1. c
2. a
3. c
4. a
5. b
6. a
7. b
8. a

Story 4
1. b
2. c
3. a
4. c
5. b
6. a
7. b
8. c

Story 5
1. c
2. a
3. b
4. a
5. b
6. c
7. a
8. a

Story 6
1. c
2. c
3. b
4. b
5. c
6. b
7. c
8. a

Story 7
1. b
2. a
3. b
4. a
5. c
6. a
7. c
8. a

Story 8
1. a
2. b
3. c
4. a
5. a
6. c
7. c
8. a

Story 9
1. c
2. a
3. a
4. c
5. b
6. c
7. b
8. a

Story 10
1. b
2. c
3. a
4. a
5. b
6. a
7. a
8. c

Story 11
1. c
2. a
3. c
4. b
5. c
6. a
7. b
8. a

23-08-98765432